PREDATOR VS PREY

HOW SPIDERS

AND OTHER INVERTEBRATES

ATTACK

TIM HARRIS

WAYLAND

www.waylandbooks.co.uk

First published in Great Britain in 2021 by Wayland
Copyright © Hodder and Stoughton, 2021

HB ISBN: 978 1 5263 1462 8
PB ISBN: 978 1 5263 1463 5

Printed and bound in China

Editor: Amy Pimperton
Design: www.smartdesignstudio.co.uk
Picture research: Diana Morris

Picture credits:
Alamy: Agefotostock 21t; **Dreamstime**: Deni Ardian 1c, 23b; Cornel Constantin 21b; Razvan Cornel 1br; Peter Waters 15t;
Nature PL: John Abbott 13b; Franco Banfi 28; Gary Bell/Oceanwide 1l, 26, 28; Oceanwide Solvin Zanki 29t. **Science Photo Llibrary**: Volker Steger 25b. **Shutterstock**: Zety Akhzar 5t; Jesse Alpert 27t; Analia26 19cr; Aottorio 9cr; Brillenstimmer 17t; 4c James van den Broek 4c; Cartoons 25c; Neophoeus S Chuang 23cl; Cornel Constantin front cover c; Ernie Cooper back cover l, 3c, 4br, 13cr; Frederico Crovettto 7b, 8, 9br; Aleksandar Dickov 19t; John Dorton 5c; Elena photo soul 4bl; H Elvin 13cl; Guy42 13t; Joan Carles Huarez 25t; Incomible 27cl; Eric Isselee 16; Nadia Kotliar 17cr; Connie Kouwenhoven 5bl; Macrovector 15cl; Magicleaf 7cl, 7cr; Andrea Mangoni 5br; Maquiladora 10r, 21cr; Ondrej Michalek 14; Marek Mierzejewski 11b; Mirrelley 25bl; Nechaevkon back cover r, 2r, 23t; Notion pic 21cl; Novarna 10l; Nuwatphoto 7t; O'Khaen 24; Suphatthra Olovedog 13cl; Poidl 3l,17b; Daniel Prudek 11t; Guiseppe R 27cr; Dustin Rhoades back cover c, 2l, 19b; Jamey Penney-Ritter 19cl; Pichit Sansupa 12, 30t; Brais Seara 18; Skifbook 20; Subphoto 3r, 29b; Kasira Suda 9t; Sunnydream 29cl; Marek R Swadzba front cover tl; Thka front cover tr;TopVectorElements 9cl, 15cl, 17cl; Udaix 29cr; VectorShow 11c; Pong Wira 9bl;Worldclassphoto 27b; Dwi Yulianto 2c, 22. **Wikipedia**: CCA-SA 3.0 Fritz Geller-Grimm 6, 31b; Jilie Metz 15b.

Wayland, an imprint of
Hachette Children's Group
Part of Hodder and Stoughton
Carmelite House
50 Victoria Embankment
London EC4Y 0DZ

An Hachette UK Company
www.hachettechildrens.co.uk
www.hachette.co.uk

CONTENTS

INVERTEBRATE PREDATORS

Invertebrates are a type of animal with no backbone. Some have soft bodies, while others have a hard, outer shell called an exoskeleton. Over 90 per cent of the world's animal species are invertebrates. These animals are incredibly diverse in shape and size, and while many eat plants, others must hunt and eat animal prey to survive.

Invertebrates exist in every habitat on Earth. Octopuses hunt in the ocean, centipedes track down prey in damp woodland leaf litter or even in our homes. Other invertebrates, such as scorpions, can survive in harsh deserts.

Almost all spiders use toxic venom to subdue their prey. Funnel web spiders are aggressive hunters that use their large, sharp fangs to deliver a dose of venom that can kill a human. Others, such as orb-weaver spiders, build beautiful webs where they sit and wait for their prey to blunder into a sticky trap.

BLUE-RINGED OCTOPUS

FUNNEL WEB SPIDER

FATTAIL SCORPION

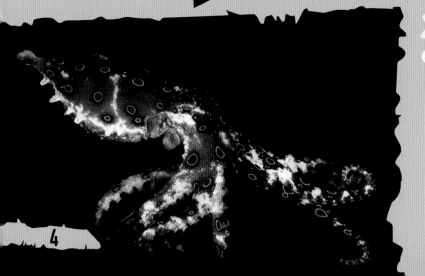

HOUSE CENTIPEDE

GOLDEN SILK ORB-WEAVER

Invertebrates form an important part of food chains. A praying mantis may catch other invertebrates, such as butterflies, but in turn may become a meal for a lizard. An unlucky lizard may become a spider's dinner.

A PRAYING MANTIS EATS A BUTTERFLY

A ROSE TARANTULA EATS A GECKO

This book examines some of the amazing ways spiders and other invertebrates hunt and kill their prey. Some use speed, others build traps or use venom and some have astonishing 'secret weapons' that spear or stun a victim. You'll be surprised by what invertebrates eat and how they attack.

SPITTING SPIDER VS MOSQUITO: SPIT

All spiders are hunters. Some of the most unusual are the spitting spiders. Found worldwide, there are many different kinds of spitting spider and most are small. Like other spiders they have eight legs, an exoskeleton and very finely tuned senses. Spitting spiders have six eyes. They hunt at night, roaming very slowly around their territory.

CAREFUL HUNTER

When a hungry spitting spider finds an insect, such as a mosquito, it approaches quietly and carefully. It comes to within 1–2 centimetres of its intended victim. Sometimes it stretches out a front leg to measure the distance to its prey. Suddenly, it spits two streams of liquid silk from its mouthparts (chelicerae). In just 0.0014 of a second the silk forms a super-strong net around the prey.

The spider then injects a dose of venom to paralyse its victim, followed by saliva, which dissolves the insect's insides. The spider then sucks them out, a bit like a sucking a drink through a straw.

VENOM: A POISONOUS LIQUID MADE BY SOME ANIMALS

SWAYS QUICKLY FROM SIDE-TO-SIDE WHEN SPITTING TO HELP THE SILK FORM A ZIG-ZAG NET SHAPE

TWO CHELICERAE FIRE OUT THE SILK AT UP TO 30 METRES PER SECOND

POOR EYESIGHT, BUT USES ITS SENSITIVE FRONT TWO LEGS TO DETECT PREY

SALIVA THAT STOPS HOST'S BLOOD FROM CLOTTING

MOSQUITO

Mosquitoes live in most parts of the world. Females have a long tube, called a proboscis, attached to their mouth. Through this, they suck the blood of mammals, birds, reptiles and amphibians for food. Although a mosquito is about the same size as a spitting spider, it stands no chance against the spider's weaponry. Its best defence is to fly away, but it is nowhere near quick enough to escape a spitting spider.

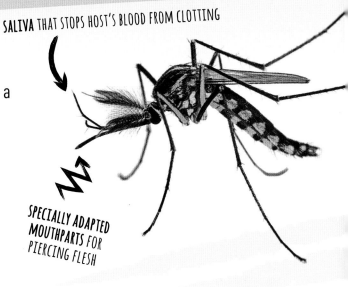

SPECIALLY ADAPTED MOUTHPARTS FOR PIERCING FLESH

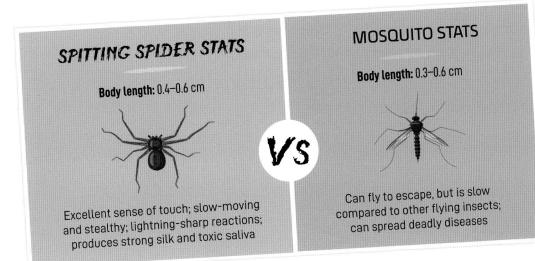

SPITTING SPIDER STATS

Body length: 0.4–0.6 cm

Excellent sense of touch; slow-moving and stealthy; lightning-sharp reactions; produces strong silk and toxic saliva

VS

MOSQUITO STATS

Body length: 0.3–0.6 cm

Can fly to escape, but is slow compared to other flying insects; can spread deadly diseases

SPECIAL SILK

The feather-legged lace weaver spider (right) has its own amazing way of using silk to trap prey. It spins silk that is almost unbelievably thin. Then it fluffs up the silk using special combs on its legs. This produces an electrostatic charge, which has the power to pull smaller prey towards the waiting spider!

TRAPDOOR SPIDER
vs BOMBARDIER BEETLE: TRIPWIRE

Trapdoor spiders are cunning killers. They dig burrows in the ground and line them with silk, which they produce in organs called spinnerets. Over the entrance to the burrow, a spider makes a trapdoor from a mixture of soil and tiny bits of plants, glued together with strands of silk. The trapdoor is hinged by silk to one side of the burrow. Since it is level with the ground, the door completely hides the burrow and the spider that lurks inside.

TRIPWIRES

The spider runs 'tripwires' of silk from the door across the ground outside the burrow – and then waits. When an insect touches a silk strand, the tripwire vibrates. The spider feels the vibration and springs into action. It pushes open the trapdoor, darts out, snatches its prey and paralyses it with venom. The victim is then dragged back to the burrow to be eaten.

LARGE FANGS FOR BITING AND DIGGING

STOCKY BODY AND LEGS FOR STRENGTH TO DRAG LARGE PREY

SPIDER SILK: VERY FINE FIBRES MADE OF PROTEIN

TRAPDOOR

BOMBARDIER BEETLE

Trapdoor spiders hunt many different kinds of beetle. If the spider is a bit slow leaving its burrow, most beetles can fly away. A beetle also has an exoskeleton, but that won't be tough enough to protect it from the spider's attack. Bombardier beetles have another defensive weapon: they squirt a very hot chemical spray at an attacker to make it back off.

CAN FIRE HOT CHEMICALS FROM ITS ABDOMEN

CAN ROTATE ITS ABDOMEN TO AIM AT AN ATTACKER

TRAPDOOR SPIDER STATS

Body length: 2.5–4 cm

VS

Excellent senses; lightning-sharp reactions; lives in a camouflaged burrow; produces strong silk and deadly venom; strong

BOMBARDIER BEETLE STATS

Body length: 2–2.5 cm

Can squirt a hot, noxious spray at an attacker; chemical spray fires in 0.1 milliseconds

TRAPDOOR SPIDERS HAVE FORMIDABLE FANGS FOR INJECTING VENOM, BUT THEY ALSO USE THEM TO DIG THEIR BURROWS.

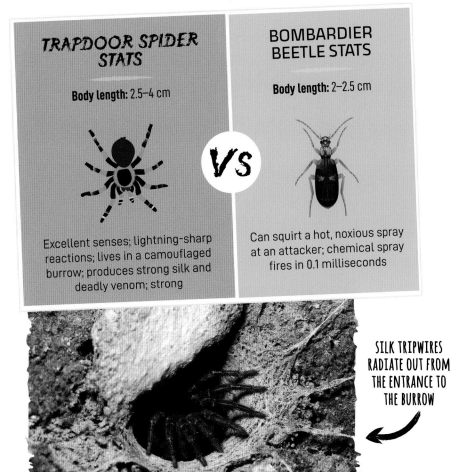

SILK TRIPWIRES RADIATE OUT FROM THE ENTRANCE TO THE BURROW

9

ORB-WEAVER SPIDER
VS WASP: ENTRAPMENT

Many spiders build webs, but female orb-weavers are master builders. Their webs are wheel-shaped traps that snare flies, wasps, moths and other flying insects. Each web may be 1.5 metres or more across. The web is made from sticky silk, which the spider produces from its spinneret organs.

NO ESCAPE

Building the web is an extraordinary achievement. The spider runs a strand of silk between branches and another strand is dropped beneath it to make a Y shape. Then the 'spokes' of the web are added. Finally, dozens of sticky spiral rings are added to connect all the spokes.

The spider takes up a central position and waits. If an insect flies into the sticky web, it can't escape. The more it wriggles to get free, the more tangled it becomes. The predator then runs to it, bundles it up tight with more silk and paralyses it with venom. It can then enjoy its meal.

LEGS ARE SPREAD OUT TO PICK UP VIBRATIONS FROM ALL PARTS OF THE WEB AND PINPOINT PREY

MANY ORB-WEAVER SPIDERS WILL EAT THEIR OLD WEB. THIS HELPS THEM TO PRODUCE MORE SILK FOR A NEW WEB.

BLACK AND YELLOW STRIPES ACT AS A WARNING TO PREDATORS

WASP

Wasps are also predators, quite capable of killing insects larger than themselves with their venomous sting. Wasps have powerful mouthparts, which can munch through other insects or even spiders. But once entangled in a spider's web, there's nothing much a wasp can do to escape.

POWERFUL MOUTHPARTS

AGGRESSIVE

VENOMOUS STING

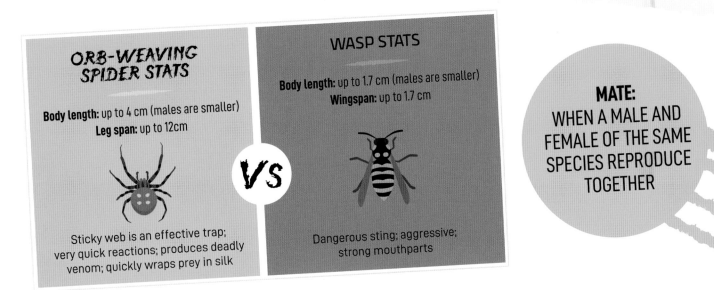

ORB-WEAVING SPIDER STATS

Body length: up to 4 cm (males are smaller)
Leg span: up to 12cm

WASP STATS

Body length: up to 1.7 cm (males are smaller)
Wingspan: up to 1.7 cm

VS

Sticky web is an effective trap; very quick reactions; produces deadly venom; quickly wraps prey in silk

Dangerous sting; aggressive; strong mouthparts

MATE: WHEN A MALE AND FEMALE OF THE SAME SPECIES REPRODUCE TOGETHER

SMALLER MALES

Male orb-weavers (far right) are smaller than females (right). They are not web builders and generally hang around the outside of a female's web, waiting for an opportunity to mate. They have to be careful though, because sometimes a hungry female eats the male!

JUMPING SPIDER
VS GRASSHOPPER: LEAPING

Many spiders feed at night, but jumping spiders hunt insects and other invertebrates by day. These spiders don't sit and wait for their next meal to come to them – instead, they walk around until they find it. They have two large, forward-facing eyes and the best eyesight of any species of spider. But how do they get close without being noticed? Well, they don't always need to ...

JUMP AND BITE

A jumping spider can leap eight times its body length to land on top of its victim. Imagine jumping eight times your height without taking a run-up! The spider then bites its victim to inject venom and paralyse it. A jumping spider doesn't have strong leg muscles, but it does something quite remarkable to achieve take-off. Super-quick, it forces blood into its back legs, making them longer, which launches the spider into the air.

MUSCLE:
TISSUE INSIDE THE BODY THAT CONTRACTS (SHORTENS) TO PRODUCE MOVEMENT

TWO LARGE FORWARD-FACING EYES HELP ACCURATELY JUDGE DISTANCE AND TARGET PREY

FOUR PAIRS OF EYES FOR ALMOST 360-DEGREE VISION

LEGS ADAPTED FOR LEAPING

JUMPING SPIDER VENOM WORKS QUICKLY, ALLOWING THIS SMALL SPIDER TO OVERPOWER PREY MUCH LARGER THAN ITSELF.

GRASSHOPPER

Grasshoppers are winged insects. Unlike jumping spiders, they have very long, muscular back legs, so they can jump to safety if they know an attack is coming. That is how they escape most predators, but a jumping spider may pounce on the grasshopper before it realises what's happening.

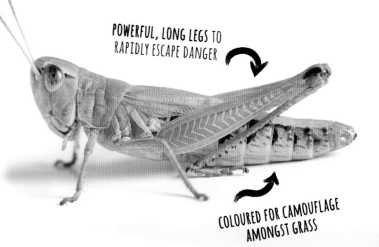

POWERFUL, LONG LEGS TO RAPIDLY ESCAPE DANGER

COLOURED FOR CAMOUFLAGE AMONGST GRASS

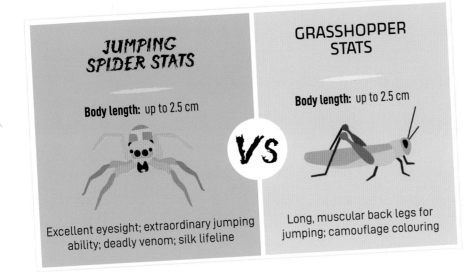

JUMPING SPIDER STATS		GRASSHOPPER STATS
Body length: up to 2.5 cm	**Vs**	**Body length:** up to 2.5 cm
Excellent eyesight; extraordinary jumping ability; deadly venom; silk lifeline		Long, muscular back legs for jumping; camouflage colouring

THIS RED-BACKED JUMPING SPIDER HAS CAUGHT A KATYDID – A RELATIVE OF THE GRASSHOPPER.

SILK LIFELINE

Jumping spiders sometimes leap from high walls and ledges. This could be dangerous, but the spiders stick a 'lifeline' of silk to the spot they leap from, so they are always attached – and can climb back to safety afterwards.

NET-CASTING SPIDER
vs MOTH: NET

Ogre-faced net-casting spiders have a long body and long, skinny legs. They rest quietly during the day, becoming active only at night. Once it is dark, a spider takes up position on a branch and weaves a square silk net about the size of a postage stamp. It shapes the net carefully with its back legs. Then the spider waits, holding the net between its front four legs.

OGRE:
A HUMAN-EATING GIANT IN MYTHS AND LEGENDS

ELASTIC NET

The net is made of coiled silk, so it can stretch easily. If a moth flies behind it, the spider quickly moves its legs and flips up the sticky net to catch the unfortunate prey.

Net-casting spiders also use their nets to snare ants, beetles, and grasshoppers walking on the ground. They sometimes drop white poo on to the ground below the net to help them target walking prey.

PAIR OF LARGE FORWARD-FACING EYES FOR ACCURATE PREY TARGETING

'HEARING' ORGANS ON THEIR LEGS HELP TO LOCATE PREY

NET-CASTING SPIDERS ARE FOUND IN TROPICAL PARTS OF THE WORLD, MAINLY IN THE SOUTHERN HEMISPHERE.

NET MADE OF COILS OF SPECIAL ELASTIC SILK

PINK-BELLIED MOTH

Moths are flying insects. Most are active at night, when they use their incredible powers of hearing and smell to avoid predators and find food and mates. Although moths are good at noticing moving things, they will not see a motionless spider lying in wait for them.

POWERFUL SENSES OF HEARING AND SMELL

AGILE IN FLIGHT

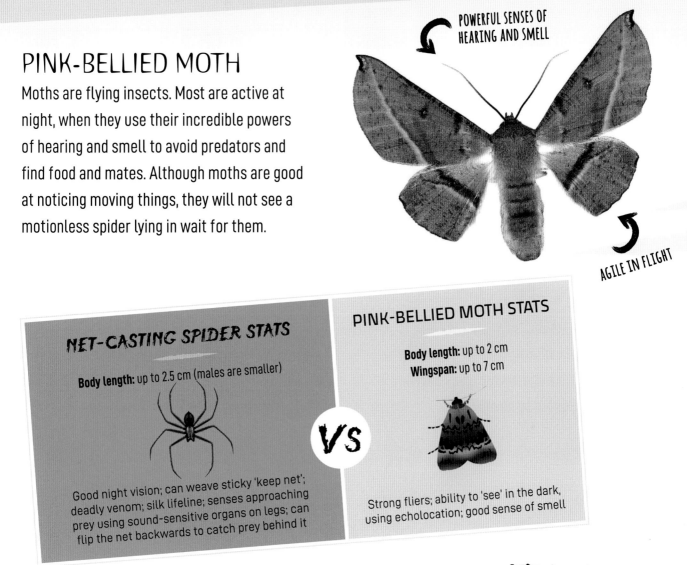

NET-CASTING SPIDER STATS

Body length: up to 2.5 cm (males are smaller)

Good night vision; can weave sticky 'keep net'; deadly venom; silk lifeline; senses approaching prey using sound-sensitive organs on legs; can flip the net backwards to catch prey behind it

VS

PINK-BELLIED MOTH STATS

Body length: up to 2 cm
Wingspan: up to 7 cm

Strong fliers; ability to 'see' in the dark, using echolocation; good sense of smell

BOLAS SPIDERS

Like net-casting spiders, bolas spiders capture prey in a similar way. They make a 'capture blob' of sticky silk on the end of a thread. They swing this at passing moths and other flying insects, a bit like an angler casts a line to catch a fish. If the spider's capture blob hits a moth, it becomes stuck and can't escape. The bolas spider then moves in for the kill.

EMPEROR DRAGONFLY
VS BUTTERFLY: FAST PURSUIT

A hunting emperor dragonfly is an impressive sight. If it spots a passing fly, butterfly or damselfly, it leaves its perch and gives chase. Accelerating to 40 kph the dragonfly will almost certainly intercept its prey, which it grasps with its front legs. They are such impressive predators that they catch over 90 per cent of the prey they pursue. Males also defend their territories and chase away insect intruders – including other dragonflies.

EATEN IN FLIGHT

Emperors eat small prey while they are flying. They take bigger insects – such as other dragonflies and butterflies – back to a favourite perch to be munched.

INTERCEPT: TO STOP SOMETHING REACHING ITS DESTINATION

INCREDIBLY AGILE IN FLIGHT

LARGE COMPOUND EYES ALLOW EXCELLENT ALL-AROUND VISION

EACH WING MOVES INDEPENDENTLY, WHICH MEANS FASTER TURNS AND MORE FLIGHT CONTROL

THESE DRAGONFLIES ARE FOUND ACROSS AFRICA AND EUROPE AND IN PARTS OF ASIA.

EYE SPOTS
ON WINGS

PEACOCK BUTTERFLY

A butterfly doesn't have any defences against a large dragonfly. It can't fly as fast as a dragonfly and doesn't have claws or teeth to fight back. The best it can do is try to trick the attacker. A peacock butterfly has an eye pattern on each of its four wings, and this may confuse a predator into thinking it is a much larger animal.

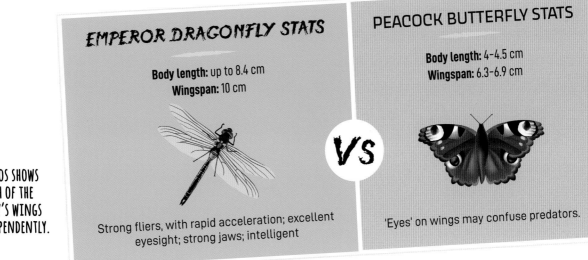

EMPEROR DRAGONFLY STATS

Body length: up to 8.4 cm
Wingspan: 10 cm

Strong fliers, with rapid acceleration; excellent eyesight; strong jaws; intelligent

VS

PEACOCK BUTTERFLY STATS

Body length: 4-4.5 cm
Wingspan: 6.3-6.9 cm

'Eyes' on wings may confuse predators.

THIS PHOTOS SHOWS HOW EACH OF THE DRAGONFLY'S WINGS MOVES INDEPENDENTLY.

SMART KILLERS

Scientists have found out that dragonflies are smart. Their brains are able to predict where their prey will fly to, helping these clever creatures to perfect their intercepting skills.

ASIAN GIANT HORNET
VS HONEYBEE: TEAMWORK

Hornets are large wasps and the Asian giant hornet is the largest of them all. Nicknamed the 'murder hornet', it hunts down and kills bees, wasps and mantises. Hornet scouts go in search of prey. They fly at up to 40 kph and can cover 100 kilometres in a day. If a scout finds a honeybees' hive, it releases chemicals called pheromones. Other hornets can 'read' these and follow the scent.

HORNETS ATTACK

Once the group of giant hornets has gathered, the assault begins. Each hornet is armed with a venomous stinger and can kill up to 40 honeybees in a minute. A group of 50 hornets can wipe out tens of thousands of bees in less than an hour. First they kill the adults that fly out to defend the hive, then they kill the larvae inside.

ASSAULT:
AN ATTACK
OR RAID

LARGE AND POWERFUL BODY

HIGHLY AGGRESSIVE

VENOM-DELIVERING STINGER

POWERFUL JAWS

HONEYBEE

If a worker honeybee senses an attack, it releases its own pheromones to warn other bees in the hive. The bees have stingers, but these won't work against the much bigger hornet. The bees have another trick, though: if a big enough group of them surrounds a hornet they can bake it to death! They form a ball around the attacker. By vibrating their muscles very fast they raise the temperature within the ball – and the hornet overheats and dies.

VENOMOUS STINGER

WORK AS A TEAM

ASIAN GIANT HORNET STATS

Body length: 4.5 cm
Wingspan: 6 cm

VS

Stinger injects venom; strong jaws chew prey; communicates with pheromones; strong fliers; very aggressive

HONEYBEE STATS

Body length: 1-1.3 cm
Wingspan: 1.5 cm

Communicates with pheromones; hive members work as team; can kill attacker by causing it to overheat

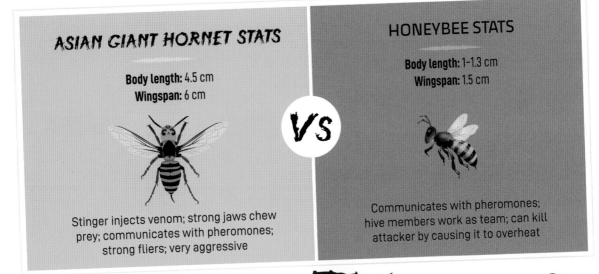

NUTRITIOUS PASTE

The giant hornets use their powerful jaws, or mandibles, to chew their victims into a protein-rich paste. They use the paste to feed their own young, back at their nest.

19

GIANT CENTIPEDE
vs BAT: STRENGTH

Centipedes are long, thin invertebrates with 15 or more body sections. Each section has a pair of legs. There are thousands of different kinds of centipede, some small and some very large. The giant yellow-legged centipede of South America has 46 legs and a pair of claws under its head that can inject venom that can be harmful to humans. As if that wasn't scary enough, this centipede grows up to 30 centimetres long and 2.5 centimetres wide.

VENOM ATTACK

The giant centipede hunts frogs, lizards, mice, small birds, deadly tarantulas and even snakes as long as itself. On the ground it coils its body around a prey animal so it can't escape, then paralyses it with venom. Then it cuts the victim into bite-sized chunks and swallows them.

Even more remarkably, the centipede can catch cave-dwelling bats. To do this, it hangs by its back legs from the ceiling of a cave and lunges down to grab an unsuspecting bat.

CLAW:
A CURVED, POINTED BODY PART FOR GRASPING OR PIERCING

VENOMOUS CLAWS – CALLED FORCIPULES – GRASP PREY AND INJECT VENOM

FLEXIBLE BODY THAT CAN TRAP PREY

STRONG FOR ITS SIZE

DAVY'S NAKED-BACKED BAT

Many bats roost and hunt in complete darkness. They find their way by using echolocation – calling loudly and listening for the echo to work out where cave walls, trees and their enemies are. This skill protects them from predators most of the time, but a lurking giant centipede may just be too quick for them.

EXCEPTIONAL HEARING

FLEXIBLE WINGS ADAPTED FOR FAST, AGILE FLIGHT

USES ECHOLOCATION

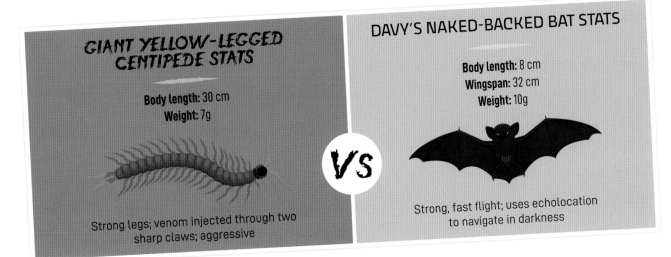

GIANT YELLOW-LEGGED CENTIPEDE STATS

Body length: 30 cm
Weight: 7g

Strong legs; venom injected through two sharp claws; aggressive

VS

DAVY'S NAKED-BACKED BAT STATS

Body length: 8 cm
Wingspan: 32 cm
Weight: 10g

Strong, fast flight; uses echolocation to navigate in darkness

UNIQUE ADAPTATION

Centipedes are found worldwide and are unique in that they are the only arthropod with forcipules. Whether big or small, these hunters are all armed with these deadly poison claws. But only a few centipedes have venom that is harmful to humans.

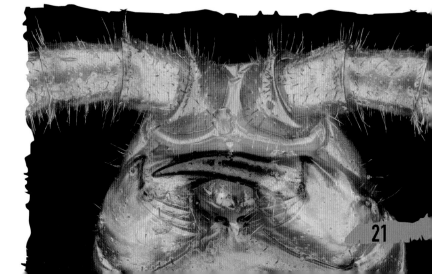

ORCHID MANTIS
VS **HOVERFLY: CAMOUFLAGE**

Mantises are unusual-looking insects with a long body and a triangular head. These insects use their front legs to grab other insects and spiders, and their other four legs for walking. Mantises are mostly ambush predators, usually standing statue-still until prey comes close, then grabbing it. Their prey won't notice them because the mantises' shapes and colours give them camouflage.

AGGRESSIVE MIMICS

Many animals use camouflage to hide from predators, but mantises use it to hide and attack – they are described as aggressive mimics.

The orchid mantis of Southeast Asian forests is an expert mimic. It climbs to the end of a twig where it imitates the shape and colour of an orchid flower, swaying gently from side-to-side as a flower does in a breeze. Flies come to visit, thinking they can drink nectar from the 'flower'. The mantis then grabs them for a quick snack.

FLOWER-LIKE BODY AND LEGS

FAST REFLEXES

SPIKY CLAWS
TO GRAB PREY

PATIENT – ABLE TO REMAIN IN
ONE PLACE FOR LONG PERIODS

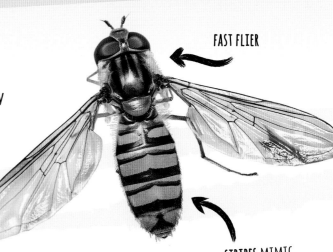

FAST FLIER

HOVERFLY

Hoverflies are brightly coloured insects that get energy from the sugary nectar in flowers. These animals are mimics, too. Their bright orange and black stripes imitate the colours of aggressive wasps, so most would-be predators stay away from them. However, if a hoverfly lands on an orchid mantis, thinking it can feed on nectar, it's in for a nasty surprise.

STRIPES MIMIC WASPS' COLOURS

MIMIC: TO COPY OR IMITATE

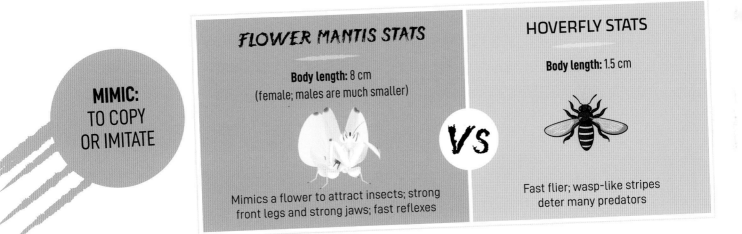

FLOWER MANTIS STATS

Body length: 8 cm
(female; males are much smaller)

Mimics a flower to attract insects; strong front legs and strong jaws; fast reflexes

VS

HOVERFLY STATS

Body length: 1.5 cm

Fast flier; wasp-like stripes deter many predators

BEAUTIFUL AND BRUTAL

Orchid mantises may look pretty, but they are lethal killers. They can change colour from pink to brown to better match their surroundings. And they can strike out with their spiny claws at a speed of around 60 milliseconds – that's fast!

23

CONE SNAIL
vs DAMSELFISH: HARPOON

Cone snails are slow-moving creatures that live among rocks or coral reefs in warm ocean waters. They live inside a tough, protective shell, which is often beautifully patterned. The snails look harmless, but looks can fool: they are actually highly venomous predators with a secret weapon.

SPEAR FISHING

Most of the time, a cone snail sits motionless, hidden under a rock or in sand on the seabed. When it wants a meal, it stretches a long, flexible proboscis towards a fish swimming nearby. Inside this tube is a tiny, hollow 'harpoon', or spear. This weapon is loaded with very powerful venom, which is strong enough to kill a human.

TAKE AIM ... FIRE!

As a fish is passing, the snail fires the harpoon from its proboscis. If the harpoon strikes the target, it pierces the fish's skin and the poison immediately paralyses it. When the snail draws the harpoon back into its proboscis, it pulls the prey with it, like an angler reeling in a fish. After it has digested the soft parts of the fish, the snail coughs up any tough scales and bones.

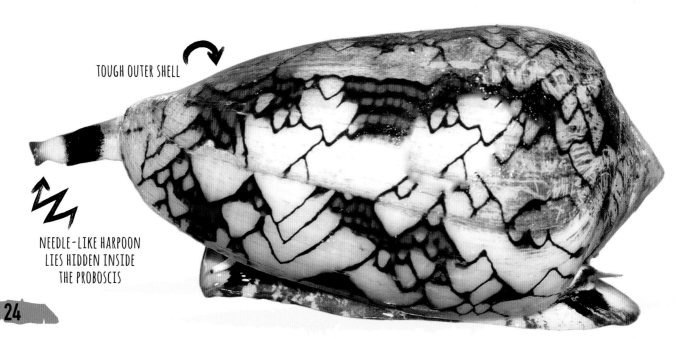

TOUGH OUTER SHELL

NEEDLE-LIKE HARPOON
LIES HIDDEN INSIDE
THE PROBOSCIS

GOOD EYESIGHT

PROBOSCIS:
A TUBE-SHAPED
ORGAN

FAST REACTIONS HELP IT TO CHANGE DIRECTION QUICKLY

CONE SNAIL STATS

Body length: up to 23 cm

Sensitive proboscis detects prey;
sharp, barbed harpoon to fire at prey;
very powerful venom

Vs

AZURE DAMSELFISH STATS

Body length: up to 7 cm

Excellent senses; fast swimmer;
can change direction quickly

AZURE DAMSELFISH

The coral reefs of the western Pacific Ocean, where cone snails are most common, are home to more than 2,000 species of fish. Wrasse and groupers are too large for a cone snail to attack, but there are plenty of smaller fish, such as butterflyfish and damselfish, to prey on. These fish have good eyesight, can detect even the slightest movements and can swim quickly from danger – but usually not fast enough to escape a cone snail's toxic spear if they swim too close.

A CONE SNAIL'S HARPOON IS SMALL BUT DEADLY. THE BARB (HOOK)
HELPS THE SNAIL TO DRAG ITS CATCH BACK INTO ITS MOUTH.

PISTOL SHRIMP
vs CRAB: SHOCKWAVE

Pistol shrimp are not large, but they are some of the noisiest animals in the ocean. They are also deadly predators. They live in tropical and subtropical oceans around the world, particularly around coral reefs where plenty of prey live. Like other shrimp, they have a tough outer skeleton – or carapace – and five pairs of legs. The claws on their front legs aren't the same size – one is much bigger than the other and this is the shrimp's lethal weapon.

BANG!

The shrimp's large front claw has a section a bit like the trigger of a gun. When it snaps shut, it creates an explosion louder than a pistol firing – hence its name. The explosion creates a powerful shockwave called a cavitation bubble. This stuns or kills any creature swimming close by – without even touching it! The shrimp then drags it back to its burrow to enjoy its meal.

ANTENNAE TO SENSE APPROACHING PREY

ONE LARGE CLAW TO TRIGGER THE SHOCKWAVE

HARD SHELL

HARD SHELL

PINCERS

RUST-SPOTTED GUARD CRAB

Crabs can certainly defend themselves from many predators. They also have tough, protective outer skeletons and pincers that can give a sharp nip. They hide from larger predators among coral, but they have no protection from the blast created by a pistol shrimp's 'trigger claw'.

TRIGGER: A SMALL DEVICE THAT RELEASES A SPRING OR CATCH

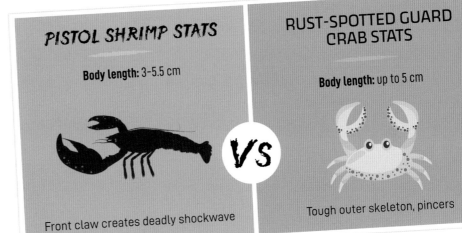

PISTOL SHRIMP STATS

Body length: 3–5.5 cm

VS

Front claw creates deadly shockwave

RUST-SPOTTED GUARD CRAB STATS

Body length: up to 5 cm

Tough outer skeleton, pincers

KILLER BLOW

There is another deadly shrimp. It is called the mantis shrimp. This colourful crustacean also stuns its prey, but with a killer punch instead of a shockwave. They smash prey with a club-like claw to break their victim apart!

JUMBO SQUID VS
LANTERNFISH: SUCKERS AND HOOKS

Jumbo squid are deepwater predators that hunt in large groups – sometimes more than 1,000-strong – in the eastern Pacific Ocean. The squid use jet propulsion to move through water at speed: they draw water into their body, then squirt it out of an organ called a siphon at high pressure to drive themselves forwards.

GRABBING TENTACLES

Squid have eight tentacles and two longer arms. Each tentacle has more than 100 suckers, each with a row of hooked teeth around it. When a squid sees prey, it swims up close and suddenly shoots out its two arms to grab it. If the victim puts up a fight, the squid holds it tight with the suckers on its tentacles. Then it pulls the victim into its sharp beak and shreds it into small pieces. Squid eat fish, but they also eat other squid – this is known as cannibalism.

RAZOR SHARP BEAK (HIDDEN IN THE MIDDLE OF WHERE THE TENTACLES MEET)

FLEXIBLE ARMS FOR GRASPING

LARGE EYES FOR SEEING IN LOW LIGHT

HOOKED SUCKERS GRIP AND TEAR FLESH

SHOOTS OUT 'INK' TO ESCAPE FROM LARGER PREDATORS

SIPHON

LANTERNFISH

These slender fish inhabit the gloomy middle depths of the ocean, down to about 1,500 metres below the surface. At night, they rise closer to the surface. Lanternfish can produce their own light from photophores in their bodies. This is called bioluminescence. They can brighten or dim their lights to match the water around them – a smart form of camouflage.

PRODUCES LIGHT
AS A FORM OF CAMOUFLAGE

CANNIBAL: AN ANIMAL THAT EATS OTHER ANIMALS OF THE SAME SPECIES

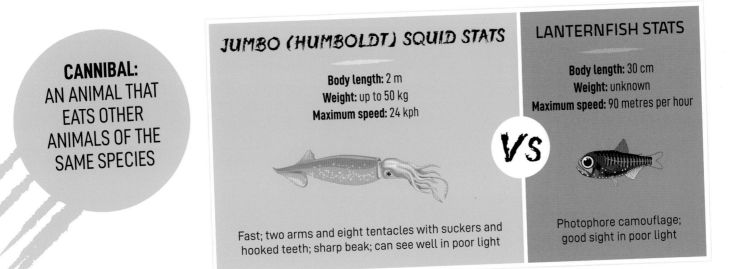

JUMBO (HUMBOLDT) SQUID STATS

Body length: 2 m
Weight: up to 50 kg
Maximum speed: 24 kph

LANTERNFISH STATS

Body length: 30 cm
Weight: unknown
Maximum speed: 90 metres per hour

VS

Fast; two arms and eight tentacles with suckers and hooked teeth; sharp beak; can see well in poor light

Photophore camouflage; good sight in poor light

COLOUR CHANGE

Squid can change colour, too. Some are able to do this because they too produce bioluminescence. Others, such as this bigfin reef squid, change colour by moving the pigments in their skin. This is called metachrosis. The squid flash colours and light when they are hunting. Scientists think they do this to communicate with each other.

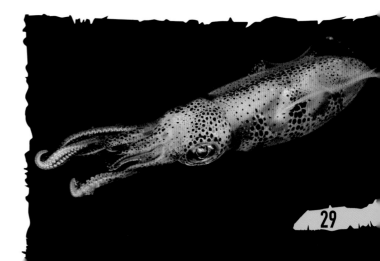

GLOSSARY

agile able to move quickly and easily

amphibian a cold-blooded animal that has an underwater larval stage, then an air-breathing adult stage; frogs and toads are amphibians

angler someone who fishes with a rod and line

arthropod types of invertebrates with jointed legs, an exoskeleton and a body that has segments; spiders, centipedes, crabs and insects are all arthropods

coral reef a hard ridge in the sea made of coral – a stony substance made from the skeletons of tiny sea animals

echolocation the location of objects using reflected sound

exoskeleton hard cover of an invertebrate's body – especially spiders, insects and crustaceans

food chain a series of plants and animals that depend on each other for food

habitat the natural home of a plant or animal

invertebrate an animal without a backbone; spiders, insects and snails are all invertebrates

mammal a warm-blooded animal with a backbone, has hair or fur at some stage in its life and is fed on its mother's milk when young

paralysed when a body – or part of a body – can't move; some spiders paralyse prey using venom

pheromones chemicals produced and released by some animals that affect the behaviour of other animals of the same species

predator an animal that hunts and kills other animals for food

predict to say or think that a specific thing will happen in the future

prey/prey on an animal that is hunted for food (noun); to hunt and kill for food (verb)

protein chains of amino acids that make up body tissues, such as muscle or spider silk

reptile an animal with scaly skin, whose body temperature is the same as the environment around it. Reptiles may bask in the sun to warm up or seek shade to cool down

senses the five main senses are hearing, sight, smell, taste and touch

spinneret an organ through which spiders (and some insects) produce silk

spoke a thread that connects the centre of a web to its outer edge; a wire that connects the centre of a wheel to its outer edge

stocky broad and sturdy

subdue to overcome or bring under control

territory an area of land defended by an animal against others of the same species

toxic something that is poisonous

vibrate to move rapidly to and fro